THE GRAND BASEBALL TOUR

```
┌─────────────────────────────────────────────┐
│           THIS BOOK BELONGS TO:             │
│                                             │
│    NAME: _____     │
│                                             │
│    CONTACT: _____     │
│                                             │
│             _____     │
│                                             │
└─────────────────────────────────────────────┘
```

The Grand Baseball Tour

Copyright © 2018 Positive Spoon

Cover photo credit: Andrew Malone

ISBN: 978-1-79-057867-2

TABLE OF CONTENTS AND CHECKLIST

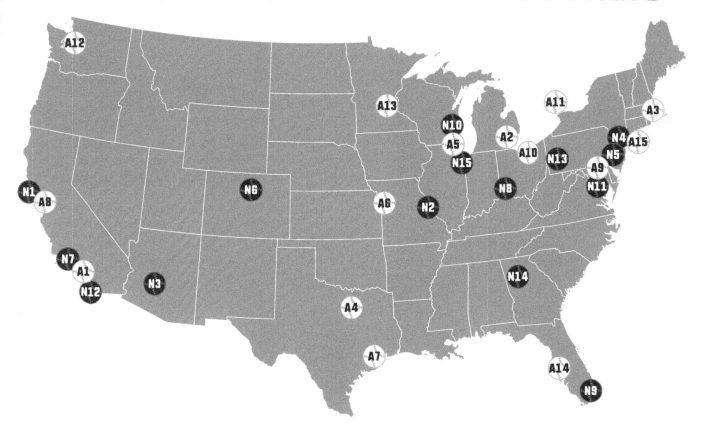

AMERICAN LEAGUE

- ☐ A1. ANGEL STADIUM...4–5
- ☐ A2. COMERICA PARK...6–7
- ☐ A3. FENWAY PARK..8–9
- ☐ A4. GLOBE LIFE PARK IN ARLINGTON............10–11
- ☐ A5. GUARANTEED RATE FIELD........................12–13
- ☐ A6. KAUFFMAN STADIUM.................................14–15
- ☐ A7. MINUTE MAID PARK....................................16–17
- ☐ A8. OAKLAND-ALAMEDA COUNTY COLISEUM...18–19
- ☐ A9. ORIOLE PARK AT CAMDEN YARDS............20–21
- ☐ A10. PROGRESSIVE FIELD...................................22–23
- ☐ A11. ROGERS CENTRE..24–25
- ☐ A12. SAFECO FIELD...26–27
- ☐ A13. TARGET FIELD..28–29
- ☐ A14. TROPICANA FIELD..30–31
- ☐ A15. YANKEE STADIUM...32–33

NATIONAL LEAGUE

- ☐ N1. AT&T PARK...36–37
- ☐ N2. BUSCH STADIUM..38–39
- ☐ N3. CHASE FIELD...40–41
- ☐ N4. CITI FIELD..42–43
- ☐ N5. CITIZENS BANK PARK.................................44–45
- ☐ N6. COORS FIELD...46–47
- ☐ N7. DODGER STADIUM......................................48–49
- ☐ N8. GREAT AMERICAN BALL PARK.................50–51
- ☐ N9. MARLINS PARK..52–53
- ☐ N10. MILLER PARK..54–55
- ☐ N11. NATIONALS PARK...56–57
- ☐ N12. PETCO PARK..58–59
- ☐ N13. PNC PARK..60–61
- ☐ N14. SUNTRUST PARK..62–63
- ☐ N15. WRIGLEY FIELD..64–65

AMERICAN LEAGUE

ANGEL STADIUM
ANAHEIM, CALIFORNIA

THE GAME

DATE: _____

SEAT LOCATION: _____
_____

WEATHER/CONDITIONS: _____
_____
_____

CONCESSIONS ENJOYED: _____
_____
_____
_____
_____
_____

STADIUM FACTS

HOME TEAM	LOS ANGELES ANGELS
ADDRESS	2000 GENE AUTRY WAY
YEAR OPENED	1966
CAPACITY	45,477
DISTANCE TO CENTER FIELD	396 FEET (121 M)
PLAYING SURFACE	GRASS
ROOF TYPE	OPEN

DID YOU KNOW?
ANGEL STADIUM HOUSES THE STUDIOS AND OFFICES OF THE ANGELS' OWNED AND OPERATED RADIO STATION, KLAA 830 AM

START TIME:	1	2	3	4	5	6	7	8	9	10	R	H	E
VISITOR:													
HOME:													
DURATION:													

AFFIX TICKET HERE

ANGEL STADIUM
ANAHEIM, CALIFORNIA

⚾ GAME DAY MEMORIES ⚾

COMERICA PARK
DETROIT, MICHIGAN

THE GAME

DATE: _____

SEAT LOCATION: _____

WEATHER/CONDITIONS: _____

CONCESSIONS ENJOYED: _____

STADIUM FACTS

HOME TEAM	DETROIT TIGERS
ADDRESS	2100 WOODWARD AVE
YEAR OPENED	2000
CAPACITY	41,083
DISTANCE TO CENTER FIELD	420 FEET (128 M)
PLAYING SURFACE	GRASS
ROOF TYPE	OPEN

DID YOU KNOW?

COMERICA PARK SITS ON THE ORIGINAL SITE OF THE DETROIT COLLEGE OF LAW, WHICH WAS ESTABLISHED IN 1891

	1	2	3	4	5	6	7	8	9	10	R	H	E
START TIME:													
VISITOR:													
HOME:													
DURATION:													

AFFIX TICKET HERE

COMERICA PARK
DETROIT, MICHIGAN

⚾ GAME DAY MEMORIES ⚾

FENWAY PARK
BOSTON, MASSACHUSETTS

THE GAME

DATE: _____

SEAT LOCATION: _____
_____

WEATHER/CONDITIONS: _____
_____
_____

CONCESSIONS ENJOYED: _____
_____
_____
_____
_____

STADIUM FACTS

HOME TEAM	BOSTON RED SOX
ADDRESS	4 JERSEY ST
YEAR OPENED	1912
CAPACITY	37,755
DISTANCE TO CENTER FIELD	420 FEET (128 M)
PLAYING SURFACE	GRASS
ROOF TYPE	OPEN

DID YOU KNOW?
FENWAY'S ICONIC GREEN MONSTER WASN'T GREEN UNTIL 1947, WHEN THE ADS WERE SCRAPED OFF AND THE WALL WAS PAINTED

START TIME:	1	2	3	4	5	6	7	8	9	10	R	H	E
VISITOR:													
HOME:													
DURATION:													

AFFIX TICKET HERE

FENWAY PARK
BOSTON, MASSACHUSETTS

⚾ GAME DAY MEMORIES ⚾

GLOBE LIFE PARK IN ARLINGTON
ARLINGTON, TEXAS

THE GAME

DATE: _____

SEAT LOCATION: _____
_____

WEATHER/CONDITIONS: _____
_____
_____

CONCESSIONS ENJOYED: _____
_____
_____
_____
_____

STADIUM FACTS

HOME TEAM	TEXAS RANGERS
ADDRESS	1000 BALLPARK WAY
YEAR OPENED	1994
CAPACITY	48,114
DISTANCE TO CENTER FIELD	400 FEET (122 M)
PLAYING SURFACE	GRASS
ROOF TYPE	OPEN

DID YOU KNOW?
SCENES FROM DISNEY'S 2002 SPORTS DRAMA *THE ROOKIE* WERE FILMED AT GLOBAL LIFE PARK IN ARLINGTON

START TIME:	1	2	3	4	5	6	7	8	9	10	R	H	E
VISITOR:													
HOME:													
DURATION:													

AFFIX TICKET HERE

10

GLOBE LIFE PARK IN ARLINGTON
ARLINGTON, TEXAS

⚾ GAME DAY MEMORIES ⚾

GUARANTEED RATE FIELD
CHICAGO, ILLINOIS

THE GAME

DATE: _____

SEAT LOCATION: _____
_____

WEATHER/CONDITIONS: _____
_____
_____

CONCESSIONS ENJOYED: _____
_____
_____
_____
_____

STADIUM FACTS

HOME TEAM	CHICAGO WHITE SOX
ADDRESS	333 W 35TH ST
YEAR OPENED	1991
CAPACITY	40,615
DISTANCE TO CENTER FIELD	400 FEET (122 M)
PLAYING SURFACE	GRASS
ROOF TYPE	OPEN

DID YOU KNOW?
THE GUARANTEED RATE FIELD SCOREBOARD PAYS HOMAGE TO THE 1960 'EXPLODING SCOREBOARD' FROM COMISKEY PARK

	1	2	3	4	5	6	7	8	9	10	R	H	E
START TIME:													
VISITOR:													
HOME:													
DURATION:													

AFFIX TICKET HERE

GUARANTEED RATE FIELD
CHICAGO, ILLINOIS

⚾ GAME DAY MEMORIES ⚾

KAUFFMAN STADIUM
KANSAS CITY, MISSOURI

THE GAME

DATE: _____

SEAT LOCATION: _____
_____

WEATHER/CONDITIONS: _____
_____
_____

CONCESSIONS ENJOYED: _____
_____
_____
_____
_____

STADIUM FACTS

HOME TEAM	KANSAS CITY ROYALS
ADDRESS	1 ROYAL WAY
YEAR OPENED	1973
CAPACITY	37,903
DISTANCE TO CENTER FIELD	410 FEET (125 M)
PLAYING SURFACE	GRASS
ROOF TYPE	OPEN

DID YOU KNOW?
KAUFFMAN STADIUM IS HOME TO THE LARGEST PRIVATELY FUNDED FOUNTAIN IN THE WORLD, AT 322 FEET

START TIME:	1	2	3	4	5	6	7	8	9	10	R	H	E
VISITOR:													
HOME:													
DURATION:													

AFFIX TICKET HERE

KAUFFMAN STADIUM
KANSAS CITY, MISSOURI

⚾ GAME DAY MEMORIES ⚾

MINUTE MAID PARK
HOUSTON, TEXAS

THE GAME

DATE: _____

SEAT LOCATION: _____
_____

WEATHER/CONDITIONS: _____
_____
_____

CONCESSIONS ENJOYED: _____
_____
_____
_____
_____

STADIUM FACTS

HOME TEAM	HOUSTON ASTROS
ADDRESS	501 CRAWFORD ST
YEAR OPENED	2000
CAPACITY	41,168
DISTANCE TO CENTER FIELD	409 FEET (125 M)
PLAYING SURFACE	GRASS
ROOF TYPE	RETRACTABLE

DID YOU KNOW?
REPLACING THE ASTRODOME, MINUTE MAID PARK IS HOUSTON'S FIRST RETRACTABLE-ROOFED STADIUM

START TIME:	1	2	3	4	5	6	7	8	9	10		R	H	E
VISITOR:														
HOME:														
DURATION:														

AFFIX TICKET HERE

MINUTE MAID PARK
HOUSTON, TEXAS

⚾ GAME DAY MEMORIES ⚾

OAKLAND-ALAMEDA COUNTY COLISEUM
OAKLAND, CALIFORNIA

THE GAME

DATE: _____

SEAT LOCATION: _____
_____

WEATHER/CONDITIONS: _____
_____
_____

CONCESSIONS ENJOYED: _____
_____
_____
_____
_____
_____

STADIUM FACTS

HOME TEAM	OAKLAND ATHLETICS
ADDRESS	7000 COLISEUM WAY
YEAR OPENED	1966
CAPACITY	47,170
DISTANCE TO CENTER FIELD	400 FEET (122 M)
PLAYING SURFACE	GRASS
ROOF TYPE	OPEN

DID YOU KNOW?
THE OAKLAND-ALAMEDA COUNTY COLISEUM WAS THE FILMING LOCATION FOR THE 1994 DISNEY MOVIE *ANGELS IN THE OUTFIELD*

START TIME:	1	2	3	4	5	6	7	8	9	10	R	H	E
VISITOR:													
HOME:													
DURATION:													

AFFIX TICKET HERE

OAKLAND-ALAMEDA COUNTY COLISEUM
OAKLAND, CALIFORNIA

⚾ GAME DAY MEMORIES ⚾

ORIOLE PARK AT CAMDEN YARDS
BALTIMORE, MARYLAND

THE GAME

DATE: _____

SEAT LOCATION: _____
_____

WEATHER/CONDITIONS: _____
_____
_____

CONCESSIONS ENJOYED: _____
_____
_____
_____
_____

STADIUM FACTS

HOME TEAM	BALTIMORE ORIOLES
ADDRESS	333 W CAMDEN ST
YEAR OPENED	1992
CAPACITY	45,971
DISTANCE TO CENTER FIELD	400 FEET (122 M)
PLAYING SURFACE	GRASS
ROOF TYPE	OPEN

DID YOU KNOW?

ORIOLE PARK AT CAMDEN YARDS WAS THE HOME OF THE INDIANS FOR THE 1994 SPORTS COMEDY *MAJOR LEAGUE II*

START TIME:	1	2	3	4	5	6	7	8	9	10	R	H	E
VISITOR:													
HOME:													
DURATION:													

AFFIX TICKET HERE

ORIOLE PARK AT CAMDEN YARDS
BALTIMORE, MARYLAND

⚾ GAME DAY MEMORIES ⚾

PROGRESSIVE FIELD
CLEVELAND, OHIO

THE GAME

DATE: _____

SEAT LOCATION: _____
_____

WEATHER/CONDITIONS: _____
_____
_____

CONCESSIONS ENJOYED: _____
_____
_____
_____
_____
_____

STADIUM FACTS

HOME TEAM	CLEVELAND INDIANS
ADDRESS	2401 ONTARIO ST
YEAR OPENED	1994
CAPACITY	35,041
DISTANCE TO CENTER FIELD	410 FEET (125 M)
PLAYING SURFACE	GRASS
ROOF TYPE	OPEN

DID YOU KNOW?
PROGRESSIVE FIELD IS STILL SOMETIMES REFERRED TO AS 'THE JAKE,' BASED ON ITS ORIGINAL NAME, JACOBS FIELD

START TIME:	1	2	3	4	5	6	7	8	9	10	R	H	E
VISITOR:													
HOME:													
DURATION:													

AFFIX TICKET HERE

PROGRESSIVE FIELD
CLEVELAND, OHIO

⚾ GAME DAY MEMORIES ⚾

ROGERS CENTRE
TORONTO, ONTARIO

THE GAME

DATE: _____

SEAT LOCATION: _____
_____

WEATHER/CONDITIONS: _____
_____
_____

CONCESSIONS ENJOYED: _____
_____
_____
_____
_____

STADIUM FACTS

HOME TEAM	TORONTO BLUE JAYS
ADDRESS	1 BLUE JAYS WAY
YEAR OPENED	1989
CAPACITY	49,282
DISTANCE TO CENTER FIELD	400 FEET (122 M)
PLAYING SURFACE	ARTIFICIAL TURF
ROOF TYPE	RETRACTABLE

DID YOU KNOW?
ROGERS CENTRE HOUSES A DISPLAY OF ARTIFACTS THAT WERE FOUND DURING THE EXCAVATION OF THE STADIUM

	1	2	3	4	5	6	7	8	9	10	R	H	E
START TIME:													
VISITOR:													
HOME:													
DURATION:													

AFFIX TICKET HERE

ROGERS CENTRE
TORONTO, ONTARIO

⚾ GAME DAY MEMORIES ⚾

SAFECO FIELD
SEATTLE, WASHINGTON

THE GAME

DATE: _____

SEAT LOCATION: _____
_____

WEATHER/CONDITIONS: _____
_____

CONCESSIONS ENJOYED: _____
_____
_____
_____
_____

STADIUM FACTS

HOME TEAM	SEATTLE MARINERS
ADDRESS	1516 1ST AVE S
YEAR OPENED	1999
CAPACITY	47,715
DISTANCE TO CENTER FIELD	401 FEET (122 M)
PLAYING SURFACE	GRASS
ROOF TYPE	RETRACTABLE

DID YOU KNOW?
DUE TO THE MILD SEATTLE TEMPERATURES, THE SAFECO FIELD ROOF ACTS MORE LIKE AN UMBRELLA THAN AN ENCLOSURE

START TIME:	1	2	3	4	5	6	7	8	9	10	R	H	E
VISITOR:													
HOME:													
DURATION:													

AFFIX TICKET HERE

SAFECO FIELD
SEATTLE, WASHINGTON

⚾ GAME DAY MEMORIES ⚾

TARGET FIELD
MINNEAPOLIS, MINNESOTA

THE GAME

DATE: _____

SEAT LOCATION: _____
_____

WEATHER/CONDITIONS: _____
_____
_____

CONCESSIONS ENJOYED: _____
_____
_____
_____
_____
_____

STADIUM FACTS

HOME TEAM	MINNESOTA TWINS
ADDRESS	1 TWINS WAY
YEAR OPENED	2010
CAPACITY	38,649
DISTANCE TO CENTER FIELD	404 FEET (123 M)
PLAYING SURFACE	GRASS
ROOF TYPE	OPEN

DID YOU KNOW?
THE TARGET FIELD FACADE IS BUILT WITH MORE THAN 100,000 SQUARE FEET OF LIMESTONE FROM SOUTHWEST MINNESOTA

START TIME:	1	2	3	4	5	6	7	8	9	10	R	H	E
VISITOR:													
HOME:													
DURATION:													

AFFIX TICKET HERE

TARGET FIELD
MINNEAPOLIS, MINNESOTA

⚾ GAME DAY MEMORIES ⚾

TROPICANA FIELD
SAINT PETERSBURG, FLORIDA

THE GAME

DATE: _____

SEAT LOCATION: _____

WEATHER/CONDITIONS: _____

CONCESSIONS ENJOYED: _____

STADIUM FACTS

HOME TEAM	TAMPA BAY RAYS
ADDRESS	1 TROPICANA DR
YEAR OPENED	1990
CAPACITY	31,042
DISTANCE TO CENTER FIELD	404 FEET (123 M)
PLAYING SURFACE	ARTIFICIAL TURF
ROOF TYPE	FIXED

DID YOU KNOW?
TROPICANA FIELD WAS COMPLETED IN 1990 BUT THE TAMPA BAY RAYS DID NOT MOVE IN UNTIL 1998 WHEN MLB EXPANDED

START TIME:	1	2	3	4	5	6	7	8	9	10	R	H	E
VISITOR:													
HOME:													
DURATION:													

AFFIX TICKET HERE

TROPICANA FIELD
SAINT PETERSBURG, FLORIDA

⚾ GAME DAY MEMORIES ⚾

YANKEE STADIUM
BRONX, NEW YORK

THE GAME

DATE: _____

SEAT LOCATION: _____
_____

WEATHER/CONDITIONS: _____
_____
_____

CONCESSIONS ENJOYED: _____
_____
_____
_____
_____
_____

STADIUM FACTS

HOME TEAM	NEW YORK YANKEES
ADDRESS	1 E 161ST ST
YEAR OPENED	2009
CAPACITY	47,309
DISTANCE TO CENTER FIELD	408 FEET (124 M)
PLAYING SURFACE	GRASS
ROOF TYPE	OPEN

DID YOU KNOW?
THE SITE OF THE ORIGINAL YANKEE STADIUM WAS CONVERTED TO HERITAGE FIELD, WHICH IS ADJACENT TO THE 2009 STADIUM

	1	2	3	4	5	6	7	8	9	10		R	H	E
START TIME:														
VISITOR:														
HOME:														
DURATION:														

AFFIX TICKET HERE

YANKEE STADIUM
BRONX, NEW YORK

⚾ GAME DAY MEMORIES ⚾

NATIONAL LEAGUE

AT&T PARK
SAN FRANCISCO, CALIFORNIA

THE GAME

DATE: _____

SEAT LOCATION: _____
_____

WEATHER/CONDITIONS: _____
_____
_____

CONCESSIONS ENJOYED: _____
_____
_____
_____
_____
_____

STADIUM FACTS

HOME TEAM	SAN FRANCISCO GIANTS
ADDRESS	24 WILLIE MAYS PLAZA
YEAR OPENED	2000
CAPACITY	41,915
DISTANCE TO CENTER FIELD	399 FEET (122 M)
PLAYING SURFACE	GRASS
ROOF TYPE	OPEN

DID YOU KNOW?

A SEGMENT OF SAN FRANCISCO BAY ADJACENT TO AT&T PARK IS NAMED FOR FORMER GIANTS PLAYER WILLIE MCCOVEY

START TIME:	1	2	3	4	5	6	7	8	9	10	R	H	E
VISITOR:													
HOME:													
DURATION:													

AFFIX TICKET HERE

36

AT&T PARK
SAN FRANCISCO, CALIFORNIA

⚾ GAME DAY MEMORIES ⚾

BUSCH STADIUM
SAINT LOUIS, MISSOURI

THE GAME

DATE: _____

SEAT LOCATION: _____

WEATHER/CONDITIONS: _____

CONCESSIONS ENJOYED: _____

STADIUM FACTS

HOME TEAM	SAINT LOUIS CARDINALS
ADDRESS	700 CLARK AVE
YEAR OPENED	2006
CAPACITY	45,494
DISTANCE TO CENTER FIELD	400 FEET (122 M)
PLAYING SURFACE	GRASS
ROOF TYPE	OPEN

DID YOU KNOW?
THE 2006 STADIUM IS THE THIRD STADIUM IN SAINT LOUIS TO CARRY THE NAME BUSCH STADIUM

START TIME:	1	2	3	4	5	6	7	8	9	10	R	H	E
VISITOR:													
HOME:													
DURATION:													

AFFIX TICKET HERE

BUSCH STADIUM
SAINT LOUIS, MISSOURI

⚾ GAME DAY MEMORIES ⚾

CHASE FIELD
PHOENIX, ARIZONA

THE GAME

DATE: _____

SEAT LOCATION: _____
_____

WEATHER/CONDITIONS: _____
_____
_____

CONCESSIONS ENJOYED: _____
_____
_____
_____
_____
_____

STADIUM FACTS

HOME TEAM	ARIZONA DIAMONDBACKS
ADDRESS	401 E JEFFERSON ST
YEAR OPENED	1998
CAPACITY	48,686
DISTANCE TO CENTER FIELD	407 FEET (124 M)
PLAYING SURFACE	ARTIFICIAL TURF (2019)
ROOF TYPE	RETRACTABLE

DID YOU KNOW?
CHASE FIELD WAS THE FIRST STADIUM BUILT IN THE US WITH A RETRACTABLE ROOF OVER A NATURAL-GRASS FIELD

	1	2	3	4	5	6	7	8	9	10	R	H	E
START TIME:													
VISITOR:													
HOME:													
DURATION:													

AFFIX TICKET HERE

CHASE FIELD
PHOENIX, ARIZONA

⚾ GAME DAY MEMORIES ⚾

CITI FIELD
QUEENS, NEW YORK

THE GAME

DATE: _____

SEAT LOCATION: _____

WEATHER/CONDITIONS: _____

CONCESSIONS ENJOYED: _____

STADIUM FACTS

HOME TEAM	NEW YORK METS
ADDRESS	120-01 ROOSEVELT AVE
YEAR OPENED	2009
CAPACITY	41,922
DISTANCE TO CENTER FIELD	408 FEET (124 M)
PLAYING SURFACE	GRASS
ROOF TYPE	OPEN

DID YOU KNOW?
CITI FIELD WAS BUILT ADJACENT TO FLUSHING MEADOWS PARK, SITE OF THE 1964 NEW YORK WORLD'S FAIR

START TIME:	1	2	3	4	5	6	7	8	9	10	R	H	E
VISITOR:													
HOME:													
DURATION:													

AFFIX TICKET HERE

CITI FIELD
QUEENS, NEW YORK

⚾ GAME DAY MEMORIES ⚾

CITIZENS BANK PARK
PHILADELPHIA, PENNSYLVANIA

THE GAME

DATE: _____

SEAT LOCATION: _____
_____

WEATHER/CONDITIONS: _____
_____
_____

CONCESSIONS ENJOYED: _____
_____
_____
_____
_____

STADIUM FACTS

HOME TEAM	PHILADELPHIA PHILLIES
ADDRESS	1 CITIZENS BANK WAY
YEAR OPENED	2004
CAPACITY	43,035
DISTANCE TO CENTER FIELD	401 FEET (122 M)
PLAYING SURFACE	GRASS
ROOF TYPE	OPEN

DID YOU KNOW?

CITIZENS BANK PARK IS POWERED WITH 100% GREEN ENERGY AS PART OF THE EPA GREEN POWER PARTNERSHIP PROGRAM

START TIME:	1	2	3	4	5	6	7	8	9	10	R	H	E
VISITOR:													
HOME:													
DURATION:													

AFFIX TICKET HERE

CITIZENS BANK PARK
PHILADELPHIA, PENNSYLVANIA

⚾ GAME DAY MEMORIES ⚾

COORS FIELD
DENVER, COLORADO

THE GAME

DATE: _____

SEAT LOCATION: _____
_____

WEATHER/CONDITIONS: _____
_____
_____

CONCESSIONS ENJOYED: _____
_____
_____
_____
_____

STADIUM FACTS

HOME TEAM	COLORADO ROCKIES
ADDRESS	2001 BLAKE ST
YEAR OPENED	1995
CAPACITY	46,897
DISTANCE TO CENTER FIELD	415 FEET (126 M)
PLAYING SURFACE	GRASS
ROOF TYPE	OPEN

DID YOU KNOW?
DURING CONSTRUCTION OF COORS FIELD, WORKERS DISCOVERED DINOSAUR FOSSILS, INCLUDING A 1,000 LB TRICERATOPS SKULL

START TIME:	1	2	3	4	5	6	7	8	9	10	R	H	E
VISITOR:													
HOME:													
DURATION:													

AFFIX TICKET HERE

COORS FIELD
DENVER, COLORADO

⚾ GAME DAY MEMORIES ⚾

DODGER STADIUM
LOS ANGELES, CALIFORNIA

THE GAME

DATE: _____

SEAT LOCATION: _____
_____

WEATHER/CONDITIONS: _____
_____
_____

CONCESSIONS ENJOYED: _____
_____
_____
_____
_____

STADIUM FACTS

HOME TEAM	LOS ANGELES DODGERS
ADDRESS	1000 VIN SCULLY AVE
YEAR OPENED	1962
CAPACITY	56,000
DISTANCE TO CENTER FIELD	395 FEET (120 M)
PLAYING SURFACE	GRASS
ROOF TYPE	OPEN

DID YOU KNOW?
DODGER STADIUM IS THE OLDEST BALLPARK IN MAJOR LEAGUE BASEBALL WEST OF THE MISSISSIPPI RIVER

	1	2	3	4	5	6	7	8	9	10	R	H
START TIME:												
VISITOR:												
HOME:												
DURATION:												

AFFIX TICKET HERE

48

DODGER STADIUM
LOS ANGELES, CALIFORNIA

⚾ GAME DAY MEMORIES ⚾

GREAT AMERICAN BALL PARK
CINCINNATI, OHIO

THE GAME

DATE: _____

SEAT LOCATION: _____
_____

WEATHER/CONDITIONS: _____
_____
_____

CONCESSIONS ENJOYED: _____
_____
_____
_____
_____
_____

STADIUM FACTS

HOME TEAM	CINCINNATI REDS
ADDRESS	100 JOE NUXHALL WAY
YEAR OPENED	2003
CAPACITY	42,319
DISTANCE TO CENTER FIELD	404 FEET (123 M)
PLAYING SURFACE	GRASS
ROOF TYPE	OPEN

DID YOU KNOW?
THE ADDRESS FOR GREAT AMERICAN BALL PARK IS NAMED FOR FORMER REDS PITCHER AND LONGTIME BROADCASTER JOE NUXHALL

	1	2	3	4	5	6	7	8	9	10	R	H	E
START TIME:													
VISITOR:													
HOME:													
DURATION:													

AFFIX TICKET HERE

GREAT AMERICAN BALL PARK
CINCINNATI, OHIO

⚾ GAME DAY MEMORIES ⚾

MARLINS PARK
MIAMI, FLORIDA

THE GAME

DATE: _____

SEAT LOCATION: _____

WEATHER/CONDITIONS: _____

CONCESSIONS ENJOYED: _____

STADIUM FACTS

HOME TEAM	MIAMI MARLINS
ADDRESS	501 MARLINS WAY
YEAR OPENED	2012
CAPACITY	36,742
DISTANCE TO CENTER FIELD	407 FEET (124 M)
PLAYING SURFACE	GRASS
ROOF TYPE	RETRACTABLE

DID YOU KNOW?
MARLINS PARK IS HOME TO THE LARGEST PUBLIC AND PERMANENT DISPLAY OF BOBBLEHEADS IN MAJOR LEAGUE BASEBALL

START TIME:	1	2	3	4	5	6	7	8	9	10	R	H	E
VISITOR:													
HOME:													
DURATION:													

AFFIX TICKET HERE

MARLINS PARK
MIAMI, FLORIDA

⚾ GAME DAY MEMORIES ⚾

MILLER PARK
MILWAUKEE, WISCONSIN

THE GAME

DATE: _____

SEAT LOCATION: _____
_____

WEATHER/CONDITIONS: _____
_____
_____

CONCESSIONS ENJOYED: _____
_____
_____
_____
_____

STADIUM FACTS

HOME TEAM	MILWAUKEE BREWERS
ADDRESS	1 BREWERS WAY
YEAR OPENED	2001
CAPACITY	41,900
DISTANCE TO CENTER FIELD	400 FEET (122 M)
PLAYING SURFACE	GRASS
ROOF TYPE	RETRACTABLE

DID YOU KNOW?
THE UNIQUE FAN-SHAPED RETRACTABLE ROOF AT MILLER PARK IS THE ONLY SUCH STYLED ROOF IN NORTH AMERICA

START TIME:	1	2	3	4	5	6	7	8	9	10	R	H	E
VISITOR:													
HOME:													
DURATION:													

AFFIX TICKET HERE

54

MILLER PARK
MILWAUKEE, WISCONSIN

⚾ GAME DAY MEMORIES ⚾

NATIONALS PARK
WASHINGTON, DC

THE GAME

DATE: _____

SEAT LOCATION: _____
_____

WEATHER/CONDITIONS: _____
_____
_____

CONCESSIONS ENJOYED: _____
_____
_____
_____
_____

STADIUM FACTS

HOME TEAM	WASHINGTON NATIONALS
ADDRESS	1500 S CAPITOL ST SE
YEAR OPENED	2008
CAPACITY	41,339
DISTANCE TO CENTER FIELD	402 FEET (123 M)
PLAYING SURFACE	GRASS
ROOF TYPE	OPEN

DID YOU KNOW?
NATIONALS PARK WAS THE FIRST MAJOR PROFESSIONAL SPORTS STADIUM IN THE US TO BE LEED-CERTIFIED GREEN

START TIME:	1	2	3	4	5	6	7	8	9	10	R	H
VISITOR:												
HOME:												
DURATION:												

AFFIX TICKET HERE

NATIONALS PARK
WASHINGTON, D.C.

⚾ GAME DAY MEMORIES ⚾

PETCO PARK
SAN DIEGO, CALIFORNIA

THE GAME

DATE: _____

SEAT LOCATION: _____
_____

WEATHER/CONDITIONS: _____
_____
_____

CONCESSIONS ENJOYED: _____
_____
_____
_____
_____
_____

STADIUM FACTS

HOME TEAM	SAN DIEGO PADRES
ADDRESS	100 PARK BLVD
YEAR OPENED	2004
CAPACITY	40,209
DISTANCE TO CENTER FIELD	396 FEET (121 M)
PLAYING SURFACE	GRASS
ROOF TYPE	OPEN

DID YOU KNOW?
THE HISTORIC WESTERN METAL SUPPLY CO BUILDING DELAYED PETCO PARK UNTIL AN ADAPTIVE REUSE AGREEMENT WAS REACHED

START TIME:	1	2	3	4	5	6	7	8	9	10	R	H	E
VISITOR:													
HOME:													
DURATION:													

AFFIX TICKET HERE

PETCO PARK
SAN DIEGO, CALIFORNIA

⚾ GAME DAY MEMORIES ⚾

PNC PARK
PITTSBURGH, PENNSYLVANIA

THE GAME

DATE: _____

SEAT LOCATION: _____
_____

WEATHER/CONDITIONS: _____
_____
_____

CONCESSIONS ENJOYED: _____
_____
_____
_____
_____
_____

STADIUM FACTS

HOME TEAM	PITTSBURGH PIRATES
ADDRESS	115 FEDERAL ST
YEAR OPENED	2001
CAPACITY	38,747
DISTANCE TO CENTER FIELD	399 FEET (122 M)
PLAYING SURFACE	GRASS
ROOF TYPE	OPEN

DID YOU KNOW?
AT THE TIME OF CONSTRUCTION, PNC PARK WAS THE FASTEST STADIUM EVER BUILT, HAVING A FINISH TIME OF JUST 24 MONTHS

START TIME:	1	2	3	4	5	6	7	8	9	10	R	H
VISITOR:												
HOME:												
DURATION:												

AFFIX TICKET HERE

PNC PARK
PITTSBURGH, PENNSYLVANIA

⚾ GAME DAY MEMORIES ⚾

SUNTRUST PARK
ATLANTA, GEORGIA

THE GAME

DATE: _____

SEAT LOCATION: _____
_____

WEATHER/CONDITIONS: _____
_____
_____

CONCESSIONS ENJOYED: _____
_____
_____
_____
_____
_____

STADIUM FACTS

HOME TEAM	ATLANTA BRAVES
ADDRESS	755 BATTERY AVE SE
YEAR OPENED	2017
CAPACITY	41,084
DISTANCE TO CENTER FIELD	400 FEET (122 M)
PLAYING SURFACE	GRASS
ROOF TYPE	OPEN

DID YOU KNOW?
WIFI AT SUNTRUST PARK IS ROBUST ENOUGH THAT EVERYONE AT A SOLD OUT EVENT COULD SIMULTANEIOUSLY POST A SELFIE

START TIME:	1	2	3	4	5	6	7	8	9	10	R	H	E
VISITOR:													
HOME:													
DURATION:													

AFFIX TICKET HERE

SUNTRUST PARK
CUMBERLAND, GEORGIA

⚾ GAME DAY MEMORIES ⚾

WRIGLEY FIELD
CHICAGO, ILLINOIS

THE GAME

DATE: _____

SEAT LOCATION: _____
_____

WEATHER/CONDITIONS: _____
_____

CONCESSIONS ENJOYED: _____
_____
_____
_____
_____

STADIUM FACTS

HOME TEAM	CHICAGO CUBS
ADDRESS	1060 W ADDISON ST
YEAR OPENED	1914
CAPACITY	42,495
DISTANCE TO CENTER FIELD	400 FEET (122 M)
PLAYING SURFACE	GRASS
ROOF TYPE	OPEN

DID YOU KNOW?
WRIGLEY FIELD WAS THE FIRST BALLPARK THAT ALLOWED FANS TO KEEP FOUL BALLS, A PRACTICE THAT STARTED IN 1915

START TIME:	1	2	3	4	5	6	7	8	9	10	R	H
VISITOR:												
HOME:												
DURATION:												

AFFIX TICKET HERE

WRIGLEY FIELD
CHICAGO, ILLINOIS

⚾ GAME DAY MEMORIES ⚾

AUTOGRAPHS

AUTOGRAPHS

AUTOGRAPHS

AUTOGRAPHS

AUTOGRAPHS

AUTOGRAPHS

AUTOGRAPHS

AUTOGRAPHS

AUTOGRAPHS

AUTOGRAPHS

AUTOGRAPHS

AUTOGRAPHS

AUTOGRAPHS

AUTOGRAPHS

AUTOGRAPHS

AUTOGRAPHS

AUTOGRAPHS

Made in the USA
Las Vegas, NV
10 April 2024

88471578R00050